TANA HOBAN

More Than One

Greenwillow Books, New York

**With special thanks
to the children of Corlears School**

10 9 8 7 6 5 4 3 2 1

Library of Congress
Cataloging in Publication Data
Hoban, Tana.
More than one.
Summary: Photographs illustrate
words that suggest more than
one of an object, animals, or
person, such as stack, bundle,
batch and heap.
1. Vocabulary—Juvenile literature.
[1. Vocabulary] I. Title.
PE1449.H54   428.1   81-1069
ISBN 0-688-00596-9   AACR2
ISBN 0-688-00597-7 (lib. bdg.)

For my parents,
who taught me the value
of independent thinking

pile
crowd
group
stack
bundle
bunch
herd
flock
team

row

group

pile
crowd
stack
bundle
bunch
herd
flock
row
team

pile
crowd
group
stack
bundle
herd
flock
row
team

bunch

herd

pile
crowd
group
stack
bundle
bunch
flock
row
team

pile
crowd
group
stack
bundle
bunch
herd
flock
row

team

bundle

pile
crowd
group
stack
bunch
herd
flock
row
team

pile
crowd
group
stack
bunch
herd
flock
row
team

bundle

group

pile
crowd
stack
bundle
bunch
herd
flock
row
team

pile
crowd
group
bundle
bunch
herd
flock
row
team

stack

crowd

pile
group
stack
bundle
bunch
herd
flock
row
team

pile
crowd
group
stack
bundle
bunch
herd
row
team

flock

row

pile
crowd
group
stack
bundle
bunch
herd
flock
team

pile
crowd
group
bundle
bunch
herd
flock
row
team

stack

team

pile
crowd
group
stack
bundle
bunch
herd
flock
row

pile
crowd
group
stack
bundle
bunch
flock
row
team

herd

pile

crowd
group
stack
bundle
bunch
herd
flock
row
team

pile
group
stack
bundle
bunch
herd
flock
row
team

crowd

flock

pile
crowd
group
stack
bundle
bunch
herd
row
team

crowd
group
stack
bundle
bunch
herd
flock
row
team

pile

bunch

pile
crowd
group
stack
bundle
herd
flock
row
team

MORE THAN ONE—and more

Have you found the <u>row</u> behind the <u>group</u>? The <u>stack</u> in the <u>bundle</u>? The <u>pile</u> behind the <u>herd</u>? Alongside the word that describes the most obvious concept are nine other collective nouns. How many of them apply to each picture? How many ways of looking at each page can you find? Is this a counting book? A shape book? A word book? Yes to all of these questions, and to many others as well. For there is more than one way of looking, and each is right!